DATE DUE

HURRY
FREEDOM

◆◆◆◆◆

JERRY STANLEY

HURRY FREEDOM

AFRICAN AMERICANS
IN GOLD RUSH
CALIFORNIA

CROWN PUBLISHERS ♔ NEW YORK

For John V. Mering

Published by Crown Publishers, a division of Random House, Inc., 1540 Broadway, New York, NY 10036

www.randomhouse.com/kids

Library of Congress Cataloging-in-Publication Data
Stanley, Jerry, 1941–
Hurry freedom : African Americans in Gold Rush California / Jerry Stanley. — 1st ed.
    p.   cm.
Includes bibliographic references and index.
Summary: Recounts history of African Americans in California during the gold rush while focusing on the life and work of Mifflin Gibbs.
1. California—Gold discoveries—Juvenile literature. 2. Afro-American pioneers—California—History—19th century—Juvenile literature. 3. Gibbs, Mifflin Wistar—Juvenile literature. 4. Afro-American pioneers—California—Biography—Juvenile literature. 5. California—Race relations—Juvenile literature. [1. California—Gold discoveries. 2. Gibbs, Mifflin Wistar. 3. Afro-Americans—Biography. 4. Pioneers.] I. Title.
F865 .S813 2000
979.4'00496073-dc21   99-57818

ISBN 0-517-80094-2 (trade)
      0-517-80096-9 (lib. bdg.)

Printed in the United States of America
October 2000

10 9 8 7 6 5 4 3 2 1

First Edition

CROWN and colophon are trademarks of Random House, Inc.

❖ CONTENTS ❖

❖❖❖

❖ INTRODUCTION

In 1841, William Alexander Leidsdorff arrived in San Francisco from New Orleans. Born in the Virgin Islands, with both African and Danish ancestry, Leidsdorff had made a small fortune as a cotton broker and merchant. It was said that he came to California after he revealed his African ancestry to the woman he was to marry and she broke off the engagement.

At that time, there were only eight black residents in the city, out of a population of less than a thousand. Leidsdorff started a schooner line between San Francisco and Hawaii, built a warehouse, and began a merchandising business. Later, he bought a steamboat with the idea of starting a service on the Sacramento River between San Francisco and Sutter's Fort, located at the present site of Sacramento. Leidsdorff's boat was small, but he went ahead anyway and packed it with a hundred friends for the maiden voyage. Battling the current of the river, the little boat took six days to reach Sutter's Fort. Shortly afterward it sank in San Francisco Bay. Undeterred, Leidsdorff bought more ships and operated the first steamboats in San Francisco Bay. He built what was then the city's largest hotel, the City Hotel, and served as city treasurer and chairman of the school board that opened the first schools in California.

In 1845, Leidsdorff acquired 35,000 acres of land along the American River, where he suspected there was gold. He was right.

On January 24, 1848, James Marshall was building a sawmill on the American River when he spotted several nuggets of gold below the water's surface. Within months, the news of gold in California had reached the east coast of the United States, and Americans were hit with gold fever. Thousands of people headed west in the gold rush of 1849, perhaps the most important event in California

San Francisco in 1846 or 1847, before the discovery of gold. This print shows William Leidsdorff's home (11) and property, including the City Hotel at the corner of Clay and Kearney streets (5) and a waterfront warehouse (9).

history. By 1860, prospectors had mined $600 million in gold, and farms, ranches, and businesses had been established. Between 1848 and the end of 1849, the population of California grew from eight thousand to a hundred thousand, and in 1850 California was admitted as a state.

Although Leidsdorff had guessed there was gold in the American River, the gold rush came too late for him. He died from typhus on April 18, 1848, just three months after James Marshall's discovery. An African American man, he is remembered as one of San Francisco's founding citizens. Not so well known is the story of the African Americans who participated in the gold rush.

When gold was discovered, four million African Americans were slaves in the South, where slavery was legal. More than a thousand were brought to California to work in the gold fields. Two hundred thousand more African Americans lived in the free states

of the North, and some of them became forty-niners (a term used to describe the people who came to California during the gold rush). They were free, but like the slaves in the South, most lived in poverty with little hope for the future. If they could find gold in California, they could use it to lead better lives—or buy a loved one out of slavery.

Few African American forty-niners kept records of their experiences in California. But Mifflin Wistar Gibbs did. He was born in 1823, in Philadelphia, Pennsylvania. Gibbs was the oldest of five children, all of whom slept in one room of a two-room house.

Sutter's Mill on the American River, photographed in 1848. James Marshall's discovery of gold here began the California gold rush.

Mifflin Gibbs. This photograph was taken in the 1860s, when Gibbs was in his forties.

Because the public schools were closed to African Americans, at the age of seven Gibbs was enrolled in the Free School, a school for non-whites. When his father died a year later, he was forced to leave school to support his siblings and his mother, who was in poor health. For the next eight years, from the age of eight to sixteen, he drove a doctor's carriage for three dollars a month.

Gibbs grew up in a world that was hostile toward African Americans. They were barred from hotels and restaurants and segregated in hospitals and even in cemeteries. When Gibbs went shopping for canvas and ropes, he was asked to leave three different stores before he found one that would sell him the items. When he used public transportation, he was forced to ride on the outside platform of the omnibus.

At the age of twelve, Gibbs observed slavery in the South, and the experience stayed with him for the rest of his life. He was driving a buggy for a lawyer who was traveling from Philadelphia to Maryland, a slave state. Along the roads in Maryland, Gibbs saw Africans in ragged clothes working on plantations. He saw children his age, who would work their entire lives as slaves and then die, never knowing what it was like to be free. He also witnessed a slave auction, where a baby was sold from its mother's arms, and he saw the mother whipped when she wouldn't let go of her child. When asked if he would like to be a slave, Gibbs answered his employer, "I would *not* be a slave! I would kill anyone who would make me a slave!"

By the age of twenty, he had a job as a handyman and was working secretly in the Underground Railroad, whose purpose was to free slaves in the South. The Underground Railroad was established by anti-slavery campaigners (known as abolitionists). They guided slaves along back roads and hid them in safe houses until they were out of the South. Gibbs escorted slaves from Philadelphia to northern destinations, from which they made their way to Canada. He helped one slave whose face had been burned with a hot poker, and he helped rescue children who were about to be sold.

Because of his work in the Railroad, Gibbs became acquainted with Frederick Douglass, a prominent African American abolitionist. He joined Douglass on several tours, during which the two spoke against slavery, often to hostile audiences. By copying Douglass, Gibbs developed a good speaking voice, and from other abolitionists, most of whom were highly educated, he learned the critical skills of thinking and writing. Gibbs shared their view that African Americans would always be treated as inferior as long as slavery existed.

The speaking tours and the Underground Railroad were the high points of Gibbs's early life. As a young man, he had acquired the skills of a carpenter, but he couldn't find much work because whites dominated the trade and excluded African Americans. He wanted to marry and raise a family. It wasn't possible without a job and money. So far in his life, he had experienced poverty and prejudice, and, other than helping slaves escape, he felt he had accomplished little.

In his autobiography, *Shadow and Light*, Gibbs said that at the age of twenty-five he became severely depressed. His people were enslaved. His life was going nowhere and there was no reason to think the future would be any different. But instead of giving up, he had a talk with himself and he heard a voice from somewhere inside him. It commanded, "What! Discouraged? Go do some great thing!" Gibbs said the inner voice gave him the strength to go to California. He would need it as he, and other African Americans, headed west in chase of a dream.

❖ ONE
We Saw a Black Man Straining

An informed person, like Mifflin Gibbs, knew that the West was extremely hostile toward African Americans. They were barred from entering Indiana, Illinois, Kansas, and Oregon. To enter Ohio, Michigan, or Iowa, they had to post a bond of up to a thousand dollars. The western states and territories wanted an all-white population and granted few rights to African Americans. Even where there weren't laws against them, they wouldn't be welcome as competitors. To add to the uncertainty, California wasn't a state yet. What if it became a slave state? What if it became a free state but barred African Americans from entering?

Frederick Douglass told Gibbs not to go to California, and Douglass's newspaper, the *North Star*, gave the same advice to all African Americans. Gibbs hesitated. Not only would he face prejudice, but he didn't have the money for the trip, didn't know the first thing about mining, and didn't know anyone else who was going to California. It certainly wasn't logic that compelled him to join the gold rush. It was more like hope born of desperation. Gibbs was captivated by the stories of blacks striking it rich in California, which he read in the *North Star* and other abolitionist papers.

After the first discovery, in 1848, sailors in San Francisco jumped ship and headed for the gold fields. Gibbs read the amazing account of two black sailors who mined $30,000 in gold in just four weeks. Even better was the story about the black man who was walking on the docks of San Francisco in 1848. A white man called to him to carry his luggage. The man gave him a stare and drew a pouch of gold from his pocket. Holding it up, he said, "Do you think I'll lug your trunks when I can get this much in one day?" The stories made California powerfully tempting to an unemployed carpenter with attitude. So what if he wouldn't be wanted in California? So what if he should be afraid? So what if other African Americans dared not go?

By 1850, Gibbs decided to follow his inner voice and take the gamble. His friends made a final plea for him to stay, but they lent him money for the trip, which he called "friendly assistance." He never said whether he had the blessing of his mother and siblings. Wearing his only suit, which was in fair shape, he left Philadelphia carrying a single suitcase containing clothes and personal items. His "friendly assistance" was hidden on his body.

San Francisco, 1851. Hundreds of ships lie abandoned in the harbor, their crews having left them for the gold fields.

While he arranged for transportation, other African Americans were already headed for California. They reached California by ocean steamer to Panama, and after crossing Panama, by steamer to San Francisco; by the Gila Trail, the overland route through Texas, New Mexico, and Arizona to southern California, and from there north to the gold fields; or by the Oregon Trail, the overland route from Independence, Missouri, to northern California.

Slaves were brought to California from the southern states on the Gila Trail. At least twelve hundred and perhaps as many as two thousand made the trip. Some owners promised freedom if slaves mined a certain amount of gold. Others pledged a percentage of gold to slaves, who could use their earnings as they wished. The promise of freedom was the best news possible—if owners kept their word.

Perhaps six hundred slaves escaped before reaching California. At night, in a wide-open country with no slave posse to catch them, they ran and headed for Mexico, where slavery had been abolished in 1824. In a hundred little dramas, they stole horses from their owners and raced through the deserts of Arizona and New Mexico until they crossed the border.

During attacks by Native Americans, slaves were often captured, and afterward they escaped to freedom. In one raid in New Mexico, Apaches captured a slave, the first African American they had seen. After closely examining his skin for two hours, they set him free.

Free African Americans from the North used the Oregon Trail to reach California. They raised enough money to travel to Missouri, where they were hired as cooks, drivers, and servants for the wagon trains headed west. Others worked their way to Missouri by herding draft animals or doing odd jobs. They came mostly from New York, Pennsylvania, and Massachusetts, and more than half hoped to buy someone out of slavery if they could get to California—and if they could find gold.

The wagon drivers, horse riders, and people on foot pushed out of Missouri with little experience in overland travel. As a result, skeletons of people and draft animals littered the Oregon Trail. Richard Cullen's party of twelve left New York in 1850. They misjudged the weather in Utah, and every member froze to death, including the party's black cook and his young daughter. Caleb Merrick, a black wagon driver for a party from Ohio, lost his life in Wyoming in 1851 when Native Americans attacked his group and wiped out the caravan. Between 1849 and 1860, cholera killed five thousand people on the Oregon Trail and dysentery killed eight thousand. Others were picked off by wolves, cougars, or the occasional rattlesnake. The Oregon Trail did not discriminate. The bones along its length included the remains of around two hundred African Americans, who lay with their employers in a final equality.

Those who made it to California experienced heat, hailstorms, swollen rivers, and meals of beans and potatoes in vinegar. Most walked the three thousand miles to California at fifteen miles a day, and when they weren't walking they were working. Hitch the mules to the wagons in the morning. Scrub the pots clean after lunch. Feed the horses and dump the trash after dinner. Wash the clothes, wash the dishes, and go to sleep on dirt under a smelly blanket. They ate by themselves, slept in their own areas, and were paid a dollar or two a week, or just food as payment for work.

African Americans were too busy working to record their trail experiences, but whites noted their presence. "On the way to California," one traveler wrote in his diary, "we saw a Negro teamster whose perspiring face was completely whitewashed with white dust. He was bent over and straining hard from the severity of his labor." Another wrote, "There she was, a Negro woman, trampling along through the heat and dust, carrying a cast iron stove on her head, with her provisions and a blanket piled on top—

all she possessed in the world—pushing on for California."

Because of the cost, few African Americans traveled by ocean steamer. It was the fastest way to reach California, but whites disliked traveling with blacks who weren't employees. James Starkey, a former slave from North Carolina, scraped together enough money for accommodations on the vessel *Pocahontas*. After leaving port—and taking Starkey's money—the captain forced Starkey into segregated quarters with the black sailors. On the steamer *Oregon*,

This 1849 print of a wagon train heading for California shows some of the hardships faced by forty-niners: overturned and broken wagons, dead or dying pack animals, and endless travel over harsh terrain.

a black man was sitting on deck enjoying the sea air. A white fire-man threw hot ashes in his face so he would vacate the seat and go belowdecks, out of sight. In some ways, the Oregon Trail was friendlier.

In April 1850, Mifflin Gibbs paid $300 for passage on an ocean steamer from New York to Panama. He spent the trip in segregated quarters with two other African Americans, and the men ate all their meals in a cramped space belowdecks. During the month-long voyage to Colón, the port where ocean steamers arrived, Gibbs occupied himself by reading newspapers and talking with his companions, who had read the same stories of the gold rush that Gibbs had read. They stayed together when they went on deck for fresh air. Of the three hundred passengers, they were the only African Americans.

There were two ways to cross Panama, by riverboat on the Chagres River, or by mule train along a trail that followed the river. The river route was faster, but when Gibbs arrived in Colón, hundreds of men were waiting for the next boat, which was scheduled to arrive in three days. Because the river route was expensive and it would mean a delay, Gibbs chose the land route. He paid $130 for the privilege of riding a mule through miles of jungle to the port of Panama City on the Pacific Ocean.

After tying his suitcase to his mule, he joined a line of approximately seventy animals and fifty travelers. The heat and tangle of vines made travel difficult; customers alternated between riding the animals and walking them around trees that had fallen across the trail. Gibbs was issued a tarpaulin to protect himself at night from mosquitoes. They were drawn to the odor of humans who hadn't bathed in days, and they were persistent. Besides totally covering the tarp each night, they would crawl underneath for a bite, making sleep difficult.

Like others, Gibbs became ill from what was called "Panama

The steamer Golden Gate, *which carried Gibbs from Panama City to San Francisco in 1850.*

fever"—malaria, spread by the mosquitoes. Gibbs's illness may have also been caused by a snakebite he suffered on his leg while walking his mule around a swamp. Whatever the cause of his fever and diarrhea, he was forced to drop behind for weeks, after which he recovered and joined another mule train. When he reached Panama City, his leg was still swollen, he itched from mosquito bites, and he hoped to never see a jungle again.

Panama City was also crowded with travelers. Sizing up the situation, Gibbs slept in a field near the waterfront with hundreds of other men. Each day he inched his way closer to the dock where passengers boarded ships for California. One of his black companions was a fugitive slave from Virginia. Another carried a map of the gold fields and a fiddle with which he hoped to earn a living. The white men in the field kept apart from Gibbs and his acquaintances, but allowed them to stay in line and hold their place each day.

After days of dirt and more mosquitoes, Gibbs secured passage on the steamship *Golden Gate*, which didn't have segregated quarters. He paid $350 for a space on deck with the other passengers who couldn't afford one of the bunks below. The passengers on deck slept in the same spot every night and ate the same meal every day: half a bottle of water, half a pound of rice, and hardtack, which resembled a crusty biscuit. The voyage from Panama City took five weeks. The entire trip from New York to San Francisco had taken five months instead of the usual three and had cost Gibbs $800.

When Mifflin Gibbs reached San Francisco in September 1850, he was in the same shape as those who had spent six months outdoors carrying cargo, herding animals, and sleeping on the ground on the overland trails. His suit was no longer in fair condition and he had ten cents in his pocket. Like other African Americans, he arrived with little more than a dream, and courage not easily measured.

❖ TWO
Our Hearts Soared to the Clouds

After arriving in California, African Americans tended to form into groups. It was safer to travel with others and easy to make friends with strangers who faced the same odds. Using wages from the overland trip, they purchased picks, pans, maps, blankets, and food. Most walked to the gold fields carrying their possessions. The deeply rutted wagon trails leading to the mining areas were crowded with thousands of men intent on getting rich.

When they reached the gold fields in the Sierra Nevada Mountains, the black prospectors were blocked from entering. William Hall and his party arrived in 1850 and were chased off by guards firing shots in the air. A man named Johnson was clubbed to the ground, and a miner known only as "Negro Dan" was found shot in the back with his possessions taken. In most choice areas, white forty-niners had formed mining associations to protect claims and share the expense of building equipment. Each excluded African Americans as well as Chinese, Mexicans, and Native Americans.

The gold rush was for whites only. The African Americans had figured as much before making the trip, and they moved on to other locations where whites weren't mining. Working in groups of twenty or more, they looked for gold in isolated locales that came to be known by names like Negro Hill, Negro Bar, and Negro Flat. There were more than thirty such locations in California, although many weren't listed on any map. During daylight hours, they scooped up sand, swirled it in pans, and studied the grains for any sign of gold. At night they slept in tents or in the open air, and when they ran out of food they ate berries or rabbits for the evening meal.

Mining associations were formed to protect claims and to share the expense of building equipment, such as this system of sluice boxes (artificial channels built to divert the flow of a river), photographed in 1851. They also confronted black prospectors, forcing them onto less desirable claims.

What a time it was for some of them. William Oliver, an ex-slave from Maryland and cook for a wagon train, found gold and bought his wife and children out of slavery. So did James Martin and Edward Jones, who brought their families to California to start a new life. In the noise and excitement of the gold rush, these events received little notice. No matter, for a newspaper couldn't convey the emotions of a man who could now buy freedom for his family.

Abolitionist papers did report the stories, while still urging readers not to go to California. One of the most widely read accounts concerned William Hall. Hall found enough gold to return to New York and marry. He spent his money on a wedding that a newspaper said had a "splendor without parallel in the history of colored society in New York." Before he returned to California in 1851 to open a billiard parlor, Hall spoke to a crowd numbering in the hundreds. His upbeat speech was called "Hopes and Prospects of Colored People in California" and caused others to head west.

An African American prospector works at a sluice box, Auburn Ravine, 1851.

Diggings at Mormon Bar, 1852. First settled by black prospectors, Mormon Bar was originally known as "Negro Bar."

Of the two thousand African Americans in California by 1852, about fifteen hundred tried to find gold. Because of the mining associations, most failed, but about two hundred succeeded. The result was an end to poverty for two hundred African Americans and freedom for about another five hundred people, bought with California gold.

Other African Americans didn't bother searching for gold. They looked for opportunities in San Francisco, by 1850 California's largest city, with a population of ten thousand. It was the main port of entry for passengers on ocean steamers lucky enough to reach California.

On September 9, 1850, Mifflin Gibbs disembarked from the *Golden Gate*, whose deck was littered with trash. He carried a banged-up suitcase and had the look of a man who needed a new life. Not knowing anyone in San Francisco, he walked the busy

View of San Francisco in 1850, the year of Gibbs's arrival.

streets, apparently without a specific plan or a vision of his future. Although stories of striking it rich had drawn him to California, he never said if he intended to mine for gold. Gibbs was articulate and intelligent and may have viewed California as just a place where he might succeed, if given an opportunity.

He quickly discovered that San Francisco might not be the place to turn his life around. Most stores and businesses displayed signs reading "No Negroes" and "No Coloreds Allowed," and whites avoided him as he made his way around the city. He wasn't surprised. With only a few pennies in his pocket, at least he didn't have to worry about being robbed.

He kept wandering until he saw several black men talking in front of a hotel on Kearney Street. It wasn't the best-looking place, but it was black-owned, and Gibbs entered. The sign above the clerk read "Board $12 a week IN ADVANCE." Gibbs said, "Had I

SAN FRANCISCO IN 1851- FROM RINCON POINT.

Photograph of San Francisco taken in 1851, shortly after Gibbs's arrival.

looked through a magnifying glass the letters could not have appeared larger. They seemed to ask, 'Who are you and do you have any money?'" Gibbs responded by spending his last ten cents on a cigar at the hotel. It wasn't the first time that he had been totally broke, but it was his first time to be broke three thousand miles from home.

He left the hotel, and after several attempts to find employment of any kind, he approached a house under construction and asked the contractor for work. The man didn't need any help, but Gibbs kept asking for just a few days' work or a few hours'. The wages were ten dollars a day and the contractor finally agreed to give Gibbs two days' work if he would accept nine dollars a day. He agreed, but there was a catch: he had to have his own tools.

Now walking with a purpose, he came upon a large tent with

San Francisco, 1849, corner of Clay and Dupont streets. Gibbs would later establish his boot and shoe business on Clay Street.

an assortment of hardware and the tools he needed. After telling the merchant that he had no money but had a job, the man looked him over and proclaimed, "All right, take them."

"I felt great relief," Gibbs said, "when I paid the merchant and my landlord on the following Saturday."

It was a start, but Gibbs's job only lasted two days. The white carpenters refused to work with an African American and threatened to strike if Gibbs wasn't fired. He was a good carpenter, at least as good as the others. The contractor didn't want to let Gibbs go and made him an offer. If he could find six carpenters with his skills who would work with him, the contractor would fire his workforce and hire Gibbs's crew. "I could not find the men he wanted," Gibbs said, "or other employment of that kind." He had tools and a few dollars in his pocket, but San Francisco wasn't any different from Philadelphia. He would have to try something else.

Most black prospectors were in the same situation and some were quick to find a way out. Having failed at mining for themselves, a few hundred went to work for white miners. Many whites believed that blacks had a special gift for finding gold and they had money to hire people to work for them. African Americans had no special gift, but they took advantage of the belief. They acted as if possessed by magic, and said they had dreams that told of riches for their employers. They earned around eight dollars a day, and by working in choice areas they found gold and kept the belief alive.

When employers mentioned these hired hands, they did so with indifference, almost as an afterthought. An ex-slave named Isadore, an elderly man, pounded rocks with a hand hammer for twelve hours a day and mined an average of seventy-five dollars' worth of gold a day for Franklin Morse. Morse remarked in passing that Isadore "was saving most of the eight dollars in wages to buy his wife's freedom." Another wrote casually, "I hired a Negro man to dig for me. He hopes to redeem his wife and seven children from slavery." The accounts totally missed the drama of the work, work that resulted in freedom.

Slaves in California hit the same wall as the black prospectors from the North. Some were allowed by their owners to go on their own to the gold fields, but the mining associations drove them off and they ended up at the locations where free blacks searched for gold. They had about as much luck, but some succeeded and bought their freedom.

Alvin Coffey was an example. A slave from Missouri, Coffey was brought to California in 1849. After mining for eight months, he earned $5,000, and by washing clothes for miners at night, he earned another $700. Coffey's owner took the money, broke his

Alvin Coffey.

promise of freedom, and brought Coffey back to Missouri, where he was sold at auction. He asked for a second chance, which his new owner granted, setting the price for Coffey's freedom at $1,500. He had the money after four months of mining and he was set free.

Slaves also earned their freedom by cooking for whites or finding other jobs. George Washington Dennis was a remarkable example. He was owned by Green Dennis, who was also his father. After they arrived in San Francisco in 1849, Green Dennis formed a partnership with others to operate the Eldorado Hotel. It didn't have any rooms and was actually a tent housing ten gambling tables that ran day and night. George Dennis was paid fifty cents a day to sweep the floor, which was made of rough lumber.

George Washington Dennis.

After working for three months, and collecting five- and ten-cent pieces that had fallen on the floor, Dennis had $1,000, which his father accepted, granting his freedom. He kept sweeping and eyeballing the floor until he earned another $950, which he used to buy freedom for his mother, who was also owned by his father. Afterward, Dennis rented one of the gambling tables and hired his mother to serve hot meals at stiff prices: five dollars for a bowl of stew, two dollars for a chunk of corn bread. They netted an average profit of $225 a day, some of which was used to buy relatives out of slavery.

At least three hundred people worked their way out of slavery in California by finding gold or working at other jobs. They earned $750,000 for their owners and used surplus wages to buy freedom for family members in the South. Meanwhile, slaves continued to arrive in California. The total stayed at about six hundred throughout the gold rush period. This included slaves who came with their owners and slaves who came by themselves to earn money for their owners and, perhaps, buy freedom.

After losing his carpenter job, Mifflin Gibbs became a bootblack. Normally, a bootblack polishes shoes. But in San Francisco, a rainy city with hundreds of horses, a bootblack first scraped mud and animal droppings from boots and then applied polish. Gibbs probably chose the job because of the pay. He worked in front of the hotels and gambling houses and earned an average of twelve dollars a day, more than he could have made as a carpenter had he been able to work at that trade.

After nine months of removing muck, he had earned nearly $2,000, ten times what he could have earned in Philadelphia. Gibbs now had hats that were in fashion, several pairs of shoes, and three new suits, which he wore after work. He looked good when he shopped for groceries and personal items in the stores where he was welcome.

Because he was friendly and because clean shoes were much desired, Gibbs came to know hundreds of whites and most African Americans in the city, including William Hall and George Washington Dennis. San Francisco's population grew larger every week, but it was a small city for the five hundred African Americans who lived there. Their neighborhood spanned about three blocks and included the hotel where Gibbs had bought a cigar when he first arrived and where he now boarded as a resident. Although his work was in the white section of town, his neighborhood was home, a place where friends could meet and talk without looking over their shoulders. Besides new clothes, Gibbs bought a subscription to the *North Star* and was known among his friends as an acquaintance of Frederick Douglass, a distinction of some merit.

The experiences of African Americans in the early years of the gold rush ranged from sudden riches to more poverty, the latter being typical. Most found no gold. A few hundred went to work for whites, while others, like Gibbs, seized opportunities in San Francisco. Among these different experiences, Moses Tucker's stands out as an example of what the gold rush could mean for those who took the dare.

A former slave from Virginia, Tucker learned to read and write in the African Methodist Church in Philadelphia. He kept a journal of his life at a place called Negro Bend, where he and others dug for gold in 1850. Another miner, named Brown, found a vein so rich that he shared the fortune. Nine men each bought someone out of slavery with Brown's gold, including Moses Tucker. He rescued his wife and baby daughter and wrote about the celebration at Negro Bend:

> Last night we gave thanks to God and the miner Brown for our Deliverance. We prayed and we cried, and every man in camp cried, practically speaking. . . . The woman called Lorena rolled in the grass, weeping and laughing at the same time. We sang to the angels and our hearts soared to the clouds. O California! O California!

❖ THREE

See Owner Inside

Whatever they were doing, African Americans in California would be affected by the constitutional convention held in Monterey in 1849. Its purpose was to gain statehood for California, which by then had a population in excess of the sixty thousand required. The delegates at the meeting might vote to make California a slave state or a free state. They might bar more African Americans from entering, or follow the lead of Illinois and Oregon, which required the periodic whipping of blacks to encourage them to leave.

All but a few delegates were deeply hostile toward blacks, and in practically every speech on the subject, they made it clear that California should be for whites only. They said, "I am against the admission of all colored men of the African race" and "I am opposed to the introduction of Negroes—free or slave" and "Let us not receive Negroes at all!" Joining in, the *Californian* newspaper insisted, "We desire only a white population in California." The editor of the *California Star* exclaimed, "Free Negroes are idle and thriftless and we do not want them in the state!" Frederick Douglass was right about the prejudice in the West.

The best way to ensure a white population would be to ban slavery. This would also make admission to the Union easier, so the delegates banned slavery. To keep California white, the convention also favored banning free African Americans from entering the state. But realizing that such a ban might upset abolitionists and delay statehood, the delegates approved a resolution asking the legislature to pass a ban *after* statehood was achieved. With fewer than seven hundred African Americans in California when the convention met, the subject of getting rid of those already in the state never came up.

California was admitted to the Union as a free state in 1850, but the first legislature failed to ban African Americans. Legislators originally from slave states were in control and they wouldn't pass a ban because it would mean no more slaves could be brought to California. Without such a ban, slaves continued to arrive; their owners pretended that they were hired hands and not slaves. This irritated lawmakers from free states, who didn't want slaves or free blacks competing with whites for work. With the two sides unable to agree, free blacks and slaves continued to arrive.

The procession in San Francisco to celebrate California's admission as a state, 1850.

Early in 1851, Mifflin Gibbs quit bootblacking and moved up a notch. He used his savings to invest in a black-owned clothing store, which had been operating successfully for more than a year. As a junior partner, he clerked in the store five days a week and basically ran it on weekends, when he learned how to order merchandise from the warehouses in San Francisco. The city's population was doubling every two years and anyone who had something to sell had buyers, even if the seller was African American. As with the bootblacking business, most of Gibbs's customers were white, and he made many acquaintances and some genuine friends.

The investment in the store brought Gibbs more money. Including wages and a share of profits, he earned around $150 a week, a considerable sum for him, although in the rest of the city fortunes were being made every day in hotels, gambling houses, and real estate. For now, he settled into a routine of working in the store and saving his money. There wasn't any use looking for a wife because the ratio of men to women in San Francisco was eleven to one, and African American women his age who weren't slaves were quickly snapped up.

By faith a Presbyterian, he attended the African Methodist Church in San Francisco until a Presbyterian church for blacks opened. He shot pool in William Hall's billiard parlor and enjoyed the Maguire Opera House, where blacks sat in the orchestra pit, segregated from whites. Outside of his neighborhood, Gibbs stayed away from places where he wasn't welcome but joined in where he could. Certain restaurants had tables against the walls designated for blacks, and bakeries had stools at the end set aside for them. If Gibbs was an outsider, and he was, he tried not to act like it. He was making money and getting ahead, and in the fluid society of gold rush California, not all whites were against him.

Like others who found no gold, many black forty-niners gave up the search after a year or so and faced reality. Their dream had ended in a cold stream containing nothing but gravel. They were in a faraway place where they weren't wanted, and they didn't have the money to go home. Tired and disillusioned, they came out of the mountains in about the same shape as Gibbs when he bought a cigar. Few foresaw the sharp turn their fortunes would take as they left their isolated locales.

Sacramento, Yuba City, Marysville, and Stockton were new towns that serviced the gold rush. When black forty-niners drifted into these towns, they discovered that there were jobs begging for applicants. Every year more people came to look for gold and there was a need for more barbers and cooks, more drivers and black-smiths, and more tailors and more people to wash clothes. The stores displayed the usual signs, "No Coloreds" and "No Negroes Allowed." It wasn't true. Businesses were desperate for workers and there were more signs reading "Help Wanted. See Owner Inside."

Who could have imagined it? The pay for ten hours of work in the gold fields was usually zero. The pay for a job in town that no white wanted was seven to ten dollars a day. All the African Americans wanted was a chance at life. In an unexpected way, the gold rush gave them that chance as the need for workers in the gold towns opened doors that were closed elsewhere. African Americans entered the businesses and hired on. For a majority of black forty-niners, this was the miracle of the gold rush: a job and a chance for advancement.

In Sacramento, William Hunter became a carpenter, Ben Peters became a blacksmith, and by 1852 another 336 had become cooks, waiters, and laundrymen. In Marysville, Edward Duplex became a barber, the Gassoway brothers became barbers, and 150 others became masons, drivers, and clerks. Hartwell Bates went to work as a cowboy on a cattle ranch in Stockton. Aaron Redding settled at the town of Hawkin's Bar and learned to be a butcher. At Foster's Bar, on the Yuba River, Sol Eaton and his wife opened a makeshift

Sacramento, 1850.

restaurant for the trade along the route to the gold fields. Customers called it Negro Tent, but they ate there and the business thrived.

The workers saved their money, switched jobs to make more money, and like Sol Eaton, some opened their own businesses. The sixty-five-ton steamer *Lawrence* carried passengers between Marysville and Sacramento on the Sacramento River. It was owned by two black men who were also the ship's cook and steward. Former slave Robert Owens worked at odd jobs until he obtained a contract to cut wood for the army unit stationed near Los Angeles. The place where he cut wood became known as Negro Canyon; Robert made a small fortune there. By 1855, African Americans in San Francisco owned four shoe stores, four clothing stores, eight wagon companies, two furniture stores, two restaurants, two billiard parlors, sixteen barbershops, two bath-houses, a lodge, twelve hotels, and a brass band. Few could have imagined it.

The gold towns transformed the lives of black forty-niners. They worked their way out of poverty by performing services that enabled the gold mines to operate, such as freighting goods to the mines and supplying horses and wagons ready to roll. And as African Americans lifted themselves out of poverty, more people became free: by 1855, at least another thousand slaves in the South were free, bought with wages earned in California.

The black forty-niners sent reports back home and it was hard to miss their pride. In 1851, the *North Star* published a letter from a carpenter in Sacramento. He wrote, "Out here a black person is just as good as a polished gentleman and can make just as much money." Another letter told readers about the black man in Calaveras County who ran a successful laundry business. When whites came for their shirts, they were told, "Pick them out of the pile yourself." The most widely circulated story concerned a conversation between a black cook and a white ship captain. In search of a cook for his crew, the captain offered the position to the black cook for ten dollars a day. The cook laughed and offered the captain a job as a cook in *his* restaurant for *twenty* dollars a day!

The gold rush also brought instances of blacks and whites putting aside prejudice and getting along together. This was especially true in isolated regions, where people met as individuals and not as members of a group. While camped along the Tuolumne River in 1849, William Miller and his partners, who were white, were invited for Christmas dinner by the black prospector William Thompson. Miller brought his fiddle and the men sang into the late hours. He returned the favor by hosting a New Year's party for Thompson, with music. In the remote town of Grass Valley, an interracial poker game started in 1852 when whites from one part of town challenged blacks from the black section of town. Although the participants kept changing, the game was played at least once a month until 1855. By then, Grass Valley had a larger population, and a mob of whites brought the game to an end.

African Americans and whites also formed partnerships and mined together in areas beyond the reach of the mining associations. For example, while prospecting along the Feather River, James Turner met a black miner from Georgia. After three days of talking, they decided to mine together and split any profits. In 1849, the Scotsman William Downie was alternating between mining and clerking in his store on the Yuba River. Downie had been thinking of forming a company to mine the upper Yuba when seven black prospectors stopped at his store for supplies.

Downieville, 1856. The town was founded by a Scotsman, William Downie, and a group of African American prospectors who formed an association to mine the nearby Yuba River in 1849.

Black and white miners, Spanish Flat, 1852.

Discussions led to a partnership with Downie, and afterward the men discovered gold and founded the town of Downieville.

For African Americans, the gold rush operated at two levels: prejudice and discrimination against them as a group, and acceptance in one-on-one relationships with some whites. This was true for Mifflin Gibbs, who led two lives. On the one hand, he succeeded as a bootblack and store clerk by establishing friendships with whites. On the other hand, when he dressed up and left his neighborhood for an errand or a walk, white strangers glanced at him from the corners of their eyes as if to say, *What are you doing here?*

Outwardly, Gibbs tried to appear as if nothing was wrong, but inwardly the hurt from rejection hadn't lessened. He still rode on the outside of the omnibus and was expected to step aside for whites on the sidewalk. Perhaps half of all businesses and all three libraries in San Francisco were closed to him, and hardly a day passed without his hearing the ugly name whites used when referring to blacks.

After four months in the clothing business, Gibbs had repaid his loan for the trip to California and had saved an additional $3,000. He was ready for his next move. In 1851, he met a former slave from Maryland named Peter Lester, and in August of that year the two became partners in a shoe store called the Boot Emporium. It was located at 165 Clay Street on the outskirts of the black neighborhood where they lived.

Gibbs surely knew about shoes. In addition, he had learned how to order merchandise and generally knew the market for wearing apparel. What expertise Lester had isn't known, but the two were equal partners, and they invested most of their savings to buy inventory for the store: hip boots, dress boots, high-heel shoes, shoes from Italy, pointed shoes, blue shoes, and cheap shoes of rough cowhide made by local manufacturers. Unlike Gibbs's investment in the clothing store, the Boot Emporium was a big gamble by two men who had only recently left the ranks of the poor.

Two years before, a California newspaper had screamed, "Free Negroes are idle and thriftless and we do not want them in the state!" A year after that, William Gwin, United States senator from California, said, "God created Negroes for slavery to serve the white race. They are not suited for freedom and they are most happy as slaves." Mifflin Gibbs and Peter Lester ignored both statements and checked the cash register for a supply of change.

❖ FOUR
Strong in the Spirit of Freedom

After moving to the gold towns, African Americans formed communities, like Gibbs's neighborhood in San Francisco. They started churches and schools, and many brought their families to California. Life proceeded. Thirty-two haircuts in a shop in Marysville. A hundred and thirty platters of steak and eggs in Yuba City. Socializing on weekends, church on Sunday, and school for children in the African Methodist Church. The gamble had paid off, but a job and money didn't mean acceptance in the gold towns or anywhere else in the state.

African Americans in California couldn't vote, couldn't hold office, couldn't serve on juries, couldn't marry whites, and couldn't go much of anywhere without drawing a stare. Blacks were valued for the services they provided, but otherwise were shunned. In time they decided to take some action on their own behalf. Step one was to fight slavery in California.

In August 1851, they held a rally in San Francisco to celebrate the abolition of slavery in the West Indies by Great Britain, which had occurred in August 1833. More than four hundred people attended, which was most of the black population of the city. Mifflin Gibbs and Peter Lester helped organize the event to coincide with similar rallies held in the East on the first Sunday in August.

Clapping their hands and moving briskly, the people marched and sang anti-slavery songs, accompanied by a band of blasting tubas and horns. After two hours of celebration, clergymen shouted prayers to the crowd asking God to speed the day when all men would be free. Such demonstrations had been held for years in northern cities, where the black population was substantial and abolitionists were organized. But it was a bold event in a city of more than ten thousand with a black population of five hundred.

A week later, the Boot Emporium opened. Gibbs said little about the business except that the high-tops and blue shoes came through the back door and left through the front to the sound of the

Peter Lester.

cash register, *ring ring ring*. The business showed a steady profit, but the real story of the Boot Emporium had more to do with freedom than with earning a living for its owners.

Gibbs said that when he first saw slaves, at the age of twelve, his "soul was stamped with a hatred of slavery." So it probably wasn't an accident that he formed a partnership with a man whose hatred of slavery exceeded his own. Peter Lester had seen slaves whipped to the point of death, and his own back was scarred from whipping. He had seen toenails pulled out with pliers to prevent slaves from running away, and he had seen escaped slaves set on fire as a warning to others not to run.

It isn't known how Lester became free. But when he came to California with his wife and daughter in 1850, he was chilled to find that slavery existed in a free state. The reminder of servitude, the marks on his back, and his craving to escape from the past made him a perfect match for Gibbs, the protégé of Frederick Douglass. Together they conspired to make a few changes in California.

During business hours, the owners of the Boot Emporium extended every courtesy to their customers, who tolerated slavery in the state. But after hours, Gibbs and Lester ran a school for leaving slavery. Slavery wasn't as rigid in California as it was in the South, and slaves weren't always under the complete control of their owners. When possible, Gibbs and Lester located slaves and brought them to Lester's house. On a typical night, dinner with four slaves might be followed by two hours of serious instruction. Their guests were illiterate, and slavery was all they had known. The idea that they weren't suited for freedom had been drilled into them since childhood.

In his strong speaking voice, Gibbs told the guests about Frederick Douglass and the Underground Railroad. Lester talked about the rights of every human being and cited himself as an example of what they could become. Slavery was illegal in California, he told them, and the state didn't have a law requiring the capture of runaways. If they ran, they could be free and they could make it on their own, as ex-slaves were doing every day. With Lester's wife at the piano, the partners ended each evening by teaching their pupils anti-slavery songs. No one knows how many ran afterward, but according to Lester, "When they left, we had them strong in the spirit of freedom. They were leaving slavery every day."

Others joined Gibbs and Lester in the struggle against slavery in California. They created a California version of the Underground Railroad, which operated out of the Boot Emporium and other black-owned businesses. While no one was looking, or, more accurately, while most were looking for gold, the network of shop owners, barbers, and tailors hid slaves until arrangements could be made to stow them on a steamer bound for Panama or Mexico.

Part of Gibbs's role in the Railroad consisted of driving a buckboard and looking as innocent as possible. Wearing the clothes of a common laborer, he made trips from San Francisco to Sacramento, where he picked up fugitives brought there by the Railroad. They came from the gold towns to the north and from the mining regions, and during return trips to San Francisco Gibbs hid them under a tarpaulin when there was traffic on the wagon trail. He rode in downpours of rain, in blistering heat, and in golden days when a breeze ruffled his floppy hat and the wagon seemed to move on its own. It was good work and the Boot Emporium wasn't neglected. Lester's wife and daughter helped out as clerks when one of the partners was away on Railroad business.

Trotting along in trips that took an average of two days each, Gibbs watched for men on horseback hired by owners whose slaves had disappeared. When the posses approached, Gibbs steered the wagon off the road in deference to them. He was always watching for posses because he knew what could happen if he was caught. A national law, passed in 1850, specified six months in jail and a fine of $1,000 for helping a slave who entered California as a fugitive. There was no penalty for helping a slave escape in California, but in reality, being caught could result in a charge of kidnapping and jail time—which could be worse than death. Gibbs was well aware of the fact that State Prison Director James Estell sometimes sent African American prisoners to New Orleans— where they were sold into slavery.

Except for boxes and the occasional stray dog, the alley behind the Boot Emporium was usually deserted at night. Gibbs drove to the back door of the store and led his passengers into a storage room with tables, beds, and an oil lamp. The occupants knew Gibbs by the time they arrived, but it didn't change their uneasiness. Seeing the partners the next morning in fine suits and shoes that sparkled perhaps gave the fugitives some hope that Gibbs and Lester knew what they were doing.

In the quiet of the storage room, the slaves could hear muffled voices in the store and the sound of the commerce that made their freedom possible, *ring ring ring*. They might stay for two days until a bribe had been paid to an employee of a ship bound for South America. Old shoes left by customers were available to them and they were given a few days' food so they could remain hidden until the ship was well out to sea. They left through the back door as quietly as they had arrived, and always at night. Gibbs was back in laborer's clothes when he twitched the reins against the horse and rode into the darkness.

The cast of characters that made the Railroad work included people from all walks of life. An African American woman named Mary Ellen Pleasant came to San Francisco from Boston in 1849 with $80,000 inherited from her husband. She opened a boarding house, started a loan business, and speculated in real estate, increasing her wealth to more than $130,000. She gave money to the Railroad and to fugitives, dined with Gibbs and Lester, and may have helped them secure slaves as dinner guests. Reverend Barney Fletcher had sold newspapers until he earned enough money to buy his wife and children out of slavery. Thereafter, he started the African Methodist Church in Sacramento, where he preached and hid runaways in the basement. A black man known only as Elijah falsified papers for fugitives who planned to stay in California, and Jeremiah Sanderson led armed raids on mining camps to liberate slaves. Town criers, such as Aaron Cobb in Marysville, walked down streets shouting news—and giving misinformation about fugitive slaves. "He was seen heading west in Mariposa County," Cobb might say, to send posses in the wrong direction.

Gibbs's friends also included white abolitionists, who had a habit of reading California's newspapers every day. Although slavery was illegal in the state, the papers carried ads announcing the selling of slaves. For example, the *Sacramento Transcript* advertised, "A valuable Negro girl aged twelve, offered for servitude. Said girl is of amiable disposition, a good washer, ironer, and cook." If abolitionists could get to the sale in time, they tried to outbid the competition.

When Charley Bates was offered for sale in 1851, abolitionists paid $750 for him and set him free. In 1853, Caleb Fay, a white lawyer, paid $1,000 for a boy from Alabama; he became a bootblack with the aim of buying his mother and sisters out of slavery. About a hundred slaves were purchased by the white abolitionists and most stayed in California.

The white abolitionists were a small minority of the population, and they paid a price for their actions. Sacramento attorney Cornelius Cole suffered losses in his merchandising business and

Abolitionist Cornelius Cole.

threats of violence after he denounced slavery. Fay's merchandising business lost clients because of his anti-slavery views. Abolitionists were sometimes physically attacked and discouraged from attending social gatherings.

The support for slavery was complicated in California, as elsewhere. Abolitionists aside, whites didn't like slavery because it meant they had to compete with slaves for jobs. But they didn't like free African Americans either. The great dilemma for most white Americans was what would become of the country's four million slaves if slavery was abolished. Where would they go—to New York, Ohio, California? Slavery was tolerated in California because it was more acceptable than the alternative—a large black population that would compete for jobs and perhaps show that blacks weren't inferior.

Yet there were whites in the state who weren't trapped by race prejudice, so African Americans had some allies. They were often in need of them. Shortly after the Boot Emporium opened, tax collectors presented a tax bill to Gibbs and his partner. The tax was required of an individual before he could vote, but since blacks couldn't vote, Gibbs and Lester saw no reason for paying. As a result, their goods were put up for auction. The hip boots and blue shoes were stacked on the sidewalk in front of the store, and more than fifty people gathered for the auction, most of them white.

At the start of the sale, one of Gibbs's white friends moved through the crowd telling people the situation and urging them not to bid. And, indeed, there were no bidders, even as the stunned tax men lowered prices to ridiculous levels. Gibbs, Lester, and some in the crowd moved the shoes back into the store and the Boot Emporium continued. The tax collectors never returned. Gold rush California had the capacity for fairness when people of different races knew each other by name.

❖ FIVE
A Modest Request

Three months after the Boot Emporium opened, the business suffered a crime that sent fear through the African American community. One day in November 1851, a white man entered the store and said he wanted to buy a certain pair of boots if Lester would set them aside for a while. After he left, a second man entered and tried to buy the same boots. The partners explained the situation, the man became angry, and to end the arguing he was allowed to buy the boots. Minutes later, both men entered the store together.

Acting upset at the loss of the boots, the first man screamed racial names at Lester. Gibbs joined his partner behind the counter but was pushed aside as the first man drew a club he had hidden and beat Lester to the floor. He kept clubbing Lester while the other man held a gun in his hand and watched for Gibbs to move. Lester was unconscious and in a pool of blood when the two men left, laughing. The owners had been set up, and the attackers left laughing because they knew they couldn't be prosecuted for a crime: African Americans couldn't testify in court against whites under any circumstances.

In April 1850, six months before California even became a state, the legislature had passed "An Act concerning Crimes and Punishments," which prohibited blacks and other non-whites from testifying in cases involving whites. Other states and territories had the same restriction, and the effect was to deny blacks the protection of the law. The law meant that Lester could have been murdered by his attacker and the crime could not have been prosecuted because the only witnesses were black. Crimes by whites against blacks, where there were white witnesses, couldn't be prosecuted either if whites refused to testify, and they could not be made to testify. For black forty-niners, the miracle of the gold rush was a job and advancement. The nightmare was little protection under the law.

To be fair, California was a violent place for everyone in the 1850s, regardless of its laws. It had a population numbering in the thousands before it had a stable government, a legal system, churches, schools, or other institutions to help bring order. The forty-niners didn't know each other and were fierce in competing for gold, jumping each other's claims, and shooting each other as well as Native Americans, African Americans, Hispanics, and Asians. The forty-niners had no attachment to California or to each other, and most planned to return home after striking it rich.

Those who did not strike it rich frequently resorted to assault, robbery, and murder. Crime was so bad in San Francisco that in 1851, and again in 1856, armed men formed vigilance committees and took the law into their own hands: they hanged suspected criminals without a trial. Between 1850 and 1853, San Francisco had twelve hundred murders, an astounding number for the size of its population. Although frequently overlooked in popular accounts of the gold rush, violence was common throughout the 1850s.

Easily identifiable, African Americans were natural targets when caught alone, as Gibbs and Lester had been. No matter the town, the newspapers carried the same stories: "A New York Negro was robbed and murdered for the $300 he was carrying"; "The Negro known as Calaveras Bill was murdered at Poverty Bar"; "Augustus Negreto was beaten and kicked in the head by George Vincent, who stole Negreto's money"; and "A white man broke into the home of a young black woman and in her presence took her money, shoes, cooking pots and can goods." Although news items, none of these crimes were punishable in court.

Even with a gash on the back of his neck and numerous cuts and

bruises, Lester recovered—after three months. He called his beating "the vicious act of a society that claims to be civilized." Gibbs called it "the work of savages," and it was a scene he wouldn't easily forget. In some ways it had been as hard on Gibbs, because he had heard Lester's screams, seen his blood splatter, and witnessed the men laughing as they left—and he could do nothing. By the time Lester returned to work, the store had a shotgun under the counter to balance out the law.

At the time of the assault, the partners knew about the law barring black testimony. Like African Americans in the gold towns, Gibbs and Lester tried to avoid situations where they might be victimized. The stones occasionally thrown at Gibbs's buckboard weren't any more alarming than a threat by a drunk who could barely stand up. But Lester's beating—in their store, in their neigh-

Gold rush justice: two men are hanged by the San Francisco vigilance committee, 1851.

borhood, by thugs who didn't want any money but were mainly out to have fun—brought a chill to the city's black population. Their very existence in California was brought into question.

How could they live in a place where their wealth and lives could be taken away any day? One answer was by being careful and being willing to live with fear. Another answer was that they couldn't go on unless they took some action to protect themselves. African Americans in the gold towns kept a low profile and went on with their lives. Following Lester's beating, African Americans in San Francisco decided to do something. The only question was what.

While Lester was recovering, Gibbs joined members of the neighborhood at a meeting in William Hall's billiard parlor. Most were business owners and workers in the Underground Railroad, and they were educated, many self-taught.

The meeting had an emotional start, Gibbs said, and for a time no one could be heard because of shouting. There were men in the pool hall who wanted to pound Lester's attackers. There were men who wanted to harm whites for all the crimes that went unpunished. Others urged restraint out of a fear of retaliation. Any action might cause businesses to suffer, and there were families and children to consider.

And it wasn't just crime that was discussed. The overall sense that they were not wanted brought bitterness and a desire to strike back: to throw a rock through every window that said "No Negroes Allowed" and to object sternly to every racial slur. In the end, the men settled on a rational approach to the main problem. They decided to petition the legislature to have the testimony law changed so blacks could testify against whites. Gibbs was appointed to write the petition.

It was a time-honored American tradition to petition the government for a redress of grievances. The American colonies petitioned Great Britain because of "taxation without representation" and the right of citizens to petition the government was guaranteed in 1791 by the First Amendment to the United States Constitution. Although denied the rights of citizenship because of their race, the African Americans in the pool hall decided to act like citizens and ask for one fundamental right of citizens, so they might lead safer lives. Gibbs wrote the petition while working in the Boot Emporium, and after several drafts he had it down to a few sentences that didn't show his anger or mention Lester in a pool of blood. Polite, but not timid, he wrote,

> To the Honorable Legislature of the State of California, We beg to protest against "An Act concerning Crimes and Punishments," passed April 16th, 1850, by which black and mulatto persons are rendered incompetent as witnesses to give evidence against white persons. This provision denies to all colored persons protection of the law, and allows the vicious and unprincipled to prey upon black people with impunity. In the name of humanity, we pray that you repeal the provision and grant to colored people the right of protection under the law.

The petition was placed on the counter of the Boot Emporium for signatures and later moved to Hall's billiard parlor and other businesses. Just in case anyone missed it, clergymen in the city's three black churches reminded parishioners to sign if they hadn't yet, and Gibbs took the document to some individuals who were reluctant to sign. They either feared losing their jobs or saw the petition as a waste of time.

After three months, the petition had been signed by nearly five hundred people, quite possibly the entire African American population of San Francisco. In its final form—signed only by African

Americans—the petition declared that they could stand up for their own rights as human beings.

A white friend of William Hall carried the petition to the state capital, Sacramento, where it was presented to the legislature in March 1852. It was met with wisecracks and racial slurs, and then rejected by a vote of forty-seven to one. The one dissenter wanted to debate the petition, even though he opposed changing the law. The other forty-seven didn't think the idea was even worth debating. If anything, the petition struck them as humorous.

Following the rejection, Gibbs was assigned to write another petition. It wasn't much different from the first one. About the same number signed, and in October 1852 it too was rejected. Six hundred people signed a third petition, including two hundred whites who were friends of African Americans. When it arrived at the legislature in March 1853, the lawmakers voted that it "be thrown out the window." Whether they continued the fun by actually doing so isn't known.

Meanwhile, crimes against African Americans continued: a barber in San Francisco was robbed at gunpoint, a laundryman in Marysville was assaulted and his equipment smashed, a dishwasher in Stockton was murdered for $200 and his horse. The people who committed the crimes weren't punished, because all witnesses were black.

The failure to change the law made Gibbs dispirited. He had hoped that if African Americans remained respectful and showed enough resolve, they might be granted the right of testimony. If they asked politely, they might be seen as human beings, deserving to live without fear. Were the hearts of white people so hardened that they could *never* change?

So far the answer was yes, and something worse. Although they made mockery of the petitions, the lawmakers weren't amused by the Underground Railroad, which was increasing the free black population by, perhaps, ten people a month. Consequently, in 1852 they enacted the most stringent fugitive slave law of any free state. For helping a slave escape in California, there was now a fine and a jail term, as there was under the national law covering fugitives fleeing to California. What made California's law unique was that it was retroactive to 1848. This meant that any ex-slave who had arrived in California since the start of the gold rush might be returned to slavery. And Gibbs could be punished for previous work in the Railroad if any fugitive he had helped was made to tell about the escape.

But the most frightening aspect to the law was that any African American in California could be made a slave. For example, by 1852, George Washington Dennis, the floor sweeper for the Eldorado Hotel, owned a livery stable worth $8,000. Suppose Dennis's father claimed that his son was a fugitive and used some bogus document as proof? Suppose the man who beat Lester claimed that Lester was a fugitive? Because of the testimony law, Dennis and Lester couldn't prove otherwise.

Sure enough, the law worked that way the first time it was tested in court. Sandy Jones had been a slave all his life. Having mined gold for two years, he was set free by his owner in California. At the age of sixty-four, his life nearly over, Jones went to work for himself, and after six months he had $3,000, the money he needed to buy his wife and children out of slavery. It was then that Jones's owner claimed he was a fugitive. Because Jones wasn't allowed to testify and present evidence of his freedom, he was returned to slavery and his owner was $3,000 richer.

After passage of the fugitive law, there was every reason for blacks in San Francisco to sit down, shut up, and mind their own business. Three petitions for the right of testimony hadn't made it to the floor for debate, let alone a vote. For helping any slave escape, prison was now a certainty, and being sold into slavery a possibility. The gold rush was turning meaner. Fugitives, some of whom had been free for years, were returned to slavery. Increasingly, California was for whites only, as its leaders had said it should be from the start of the gold rush.

But Gibbs and his associates in the Railroad carried on. In the summer of 1853, Gibbs was returning from Sacramento when his buckboard was stopped by a posse charged with enforcing the fugitive law. He was made to present proof of his freedom—his birth certificate, which he had learned to carry at all times when working in the Railroad in Philadelphia. Fortunately, he had been warned about the men. After they rode off, he doubled back to the woods, where he had hidden the thirteen-year-old boy he was helping to escape. They sped away.

Once the storage room was occupied, Gibbs returned to fitting customers with shoes and gave no indication of the side business in the next room. When white friends were in the store, there was no fear of crime and the partners focused on commerce. The gold rush was still going full tilt. The Boot Emporium grabbed its share.

By 1853, two years after Lester's beating, the store was shipping shoes to southern California, Oregon, and Nevada, and had two employees, a stockman and an additional clerk. Still neatly dressed and courteous to customers, Gibbs and Lester seemed like ordinary people trying to get ahead. Other than money, not much in their lives had changed. They still had dinner guests twice a week, and every August they marched for freedom, wearing their best suits and shoes that sparkled, and holding their heads high.

❖ SIX
Assemble Yourselves Together

After the third petition failed in 1853, African Americans in San Francisco hired lawyers to fight the testimony law in court. The Boot Emporium donated $5,000 to the cause while other businesses kicked in $20,000 to cover legal fees. Gibbs and Lester took turns attending the trials with others to show resolve.

Because of the rising violence against blacks—and because of their presence in court—some judges ignored the law and allowed black testimony. In 1853, the black barber Edward Duplex testified against a white assailant, who was convicted of robbery. Weeks later, a woman from Stockton named Ellen presented evidence of her freedom and she wasn't returned to slavery. Although the victories were few in number, they raised the spirits of Gibbs and the others. "The judges were right to violate the law," Gibbs said, "and they were an encouragement in our struggle for testimony."

Then, just as swiftly, the courts killed black testimony. In 1854, a white man named Hall was convicted of murder on the testimony of Chinese witnesses. The lower court allowed the testimony because Chinese weren't mentioned in the law barring certain groups from testifying against whites. The case was appealed to the California Supreme Court.

In the ruling that resulted, *The People* v. *Hall*, the California Supreme Court said that since Chinese and Native Americans had the same ancestors in Asia, the Chinese had the same status as Native Americans. Since Native Americans couldn't testify under the 1850 law, Chinese couldn't either. The murder conviction was overturned; the testimony law was upheld. From now on, judges needn't bother hearing black witnesses, as the cases would be overturned. First the legislature, and now the highest court in

California, had said "no" to the right of testimony.

African Americans in the gold towns didn't necessarily know about the fight for testimony or the defeat in court. The three petitions weren't mentioned in newspapers, even as curious items, and it wasn't news that African Americans, Native Americans, Chinese, and the insane couldn't testify against whites. Had the court ruled otherwise, it would have made headline news. As it was, only African Americans in San Francisco felt the sting of defeat and a growing sense of hopelessness.

Following the ruling, Gibbs and his friends held a meeting in the newly established San Francisco Atheneum, which had replaced the pool hall as a meeting place. Established by Gibbs, Lester, William Hall, and nine others, the Atheneum was an institution for learning. It was part of a two-story building; a saloon occupied the first floor and the Atheneum the second. Membership dues were used for subscriptions to abolitionist papers and to build a library of a thousand books on subjects ranging from the manufacture of leather to the abolition of slavery. The Atheneum had more than a hundred members, including George Washington Dennis and James Starkey, the man forced into segregated quarters on the ocean steamer *Pocahontas*.

Gibbs and Lester were the main speakers at the meeting following the defeat in the Supreme Court. It was hard to say which was more upset. After three petitions and all the money spent in court, Gibbs declared, "We have failed to change a single mind! God knows we have tried! We should go and leave this place! Leave, before it is too late!" He suggested that members migrate to Nicaragua or Panama, where there was protection under the law for everyone.

Lester answered with an outburst, which may have stunned some in the meeting, the partners being so close. First, leaving would mean the end of the Underground Railroad and, he said, "a victory for slavery." The scars on Lester's back were talking, Gibbs understood; his memory of seeing slavery in Maryland could never be the same as having been a slave there. Lester cited the same court decision and failure of the petitions as reasons for staying. The fact that nothing had changed in three years was why they needed to stay and fight. "It is justice for our people that we seek!" he shouted. "To leave would be an act of cowardice!"

Gibbs said that the debate on the two ideas "raged like a storm upon the sea." He probably wasn't surprised that Lester wanted to stay, and when that became the sentiment of the meeting, Gibbs joined the majority. "The Negro community," he said with some pride, "was resolved to have the fight go on. We could not live in a place where our lives and property were threatened daily. We were determined to fight on and try something new."

What they tried was to meet publicly and have all black forty-niners—all five thousand—raise their voices collectively. In September 1855, the Atheneum issued a call for the "First State Convention of Colored Citizens of California." It was to be held starting November 21 in Sacramento, the halfway point between San Francisco and the gold towns, and where the legislature met. Written by Gibbs, Lester, and Hall, the call to the convention read,

> Brethren—your state and condition in California is one of
> social and political degradation; one that is unbecoming
> of a free and enlightened people. Since you have left your
> friends and homes in the Atlantic States, and migrated to
> the shores of the Pacific, with hopes of bettering your
> condition, you have been met with a continuous series of
> outrages, injustices, and unmitigated wrongs. By "An Act
> concerning Crimes and Punishments," which passed into
> law on April 16, 1850, we are declared incompetent to give
> evidence against white persons in a court of law. This law was

unjustly imposed upon us and denies us our common
humanity.

In the enlightened spirit of the age in which we live,
and the great duty we owe ourselves and the generations
yet to come, we call upon you to lay aside your various
vocations and assemble yourselves together . . . for the
purpose of securing our right to testimony.

Gibbs's buckboard carried the partners to Sacramento. It was a
familiar road, but there was no hiding under the tarp on this trip.
As they arrived, white ashes from a brush fire fell on the state capital, causing newspapers to write humorously about "The Colored
Snow Storm."

The forty-nine delegates to the three-day convention came
almost entirely from Sacramento and San Francisco. Marysville,
Yuba City, and other gold towns sent few representatives because
African Americans there feared a loss of business and jobs. They
had families and money, and although they lived in fear, the trade-
off was worth it to them.

The convention was held in Barney Fletcher's African
Methodist Church, a key link in the Underground Railroad. Gibbs
and Lester sat in the third row as Jeremiah Sanderson, the slave
raider, gaveled the meeting to order.

The first business was to choose a chairman. Both Gibbs and his
partner voted for the obvious choice, William Yates, a tall, muscu-
lar man described as "articulate and deliberate in thought." Born a
slave, Yates bought his freedom by working on the side as a carpenter, and after purchasing his wife and children, he moved the
family to California in 1851. By 1855, he was one of the best-paid
stewards on the luxury steamers operating in San Francisco Bay.
Gibbs knew him from cruises on the bay, which he was fond of taking for recreation, and as an Atheneum member. Slavery had

toughened Yates, and his size and muscle gave him the look of a leader.

The first day was devoted to keeping order, which was no easy task. Yates banged his gavel "no" at every attempt to distract the convention: "no" to the idea of creating a black-owned bank, "no" to a discussion of the latest bill to stop blacks from entering California, "no" to the right to vote, "no" to access to schools, "no" to a motion condemning slavery. Resolutions on these subjects would make good reading in the *North Star* but wouldn't help the cause in California. "We have but one purpose," Yates said in telling delegates to stay focused on the testimony law. Gibbs didn't speak during the first day.

But on the second day, Gibbs rose and displayed the skills he had learned from Frederick Douglass and other abolitionists. At issue was the wording of the resolution asking for the right to give testimony. Jonas Townsend, a journalist and founding member of the Atheneum, argued it should say they were being denied testimony because of race prejudice. This was true, of course, but saying it, Gibbs declared, would only push whites away, and white support was needed for success. He argued that they should appeal to whites on the grounds that once the law was changed, blacks could testify for whites when *they* were victims of crimes.

Following another outburst from Townsend, Gibbs urged that they emphasize their education and wealth, which qualified them to testify. William Newby, a veteran of conventions in the East and highly respected, sided with Gibbs and helped him gain support. "We are an oppressed people," Newby said, "the victims of a bitter race prejudice, which we are seeking to overcome. In appealing to our oppressors, we desire to do so in a manner that will have weight."

When the resolution was approved on the third day, it said nothing about blacks being murdered or about racism. Instead, it stated that the 4,815 African Americans in the state had a combined wealth of $2,423,000. The resolution argued that wealth and intelligence qualified them to testify, and that this would benefit whites as well.

On the ride back to San Francisco, Gibbs took comfort in the work of the convention, which had produced a suitable appeal to whites. He was also pleased that Jonas Townsend had been chosen to deliver the closing address, where Townsend's fire was appropriate. A reporter said that he started with an "even tone and his voice rose to a climax." At a time when it was normal to deny basic human rights because of race, Townsend thundered,

> We again call upon you to regard our condition in the State of California. We point with pride to the character we maintain in your midst, for integrity, industry, and thrift. . . .
>
> You require us to be good citizens while seeking to degrade us. You ask why we are not more intelligent? You receive our money to educate your children and then refuse to admit our children into the common schools. . . .
>
> Most of the colored men in this state can read and write and conduct industry, without hurting the interests of whites. We beseech you to let the colored people of this great state testify to protect their lives and property as white people do! Our Divine Father has seen fit to create us with a darker complexion, but we are still part of Humanity! We are still human beings! We ask that you hear our plea—in the name of God Almighty!

❖ SEVEN
When Each Heart Was Innocent

The resolution adopted by the convention would be presented to the legislature in 1856 as the fourth petition for testimony. Following the convention, Jonas Townsend rode a horse through the mining towns in the north, telling workmen about the meeting and collecting signatures for the petition. Barney Fletcher and Jeremiah Sanderson covered Sacramento while Gibbs, Lester, and Hall worked San Francisco. The fourth campaign, Gibbs said, "had the effect of arousing the timid element in the Negro community outside of San Francisco, and all signed willingly." Most did and became part of something larger than their own lives.

The fourth petition wasn't like the first three in another respect. Gibbs had put his finger on the key to success, gaining white support, and the main effort of this petition was to secure as many signatures from whites as possible. After their white friends had signed, the activists would have to leave the safety of the neighborhood and approach strangers. After six years of receiving stares from them, Mifflin Gibbs would have to walk up to the strangers and start a conversation. The Underground Railroad was easier. If there ever was a time when Gibbs needed inner strength, this was it.

Imagine him entering a clothing store with a sign in the window reading "No Negroes." He would take off his hat upon entering, approach the owner behind the counter, and smile to customers if it seemed the right thing to do at the moment. "I beg you, sir, to have just a moment of your time," he might start, "for a cause that will help your race as well as mine." Imagine Lester, with his gleaming scar, doing the same. Most of the time they were ordered out. If not, the conversation was short, while customers stared and whispered disapproval. The men took the scorn and moved on to the next store, hoping for a better result. Gibbs worked for three months at the task.

By now, the struggle for testimony had become public and was covered in newspapers. Adopting Gibbs's idea, a few favored changing the law so blacks could help whites in crimes where whites were victims. The papers offered examples of how whites could benefit.

The *San Francisco Chronicle* said:

> Suppose there was a gentleman who had a faithful servant. The servant had been a family slave whom the master trusted with his life and property. If a white thief should break into his house and murder his wife or child and rob his place and the black servant should be the only one to see it, the master could not bring the culprit to justice.

The *Alta California* said:

> We have no love for the Negro. He is degraded and not wanted in this great state. The Negro's evidence should not carry as much weight as a white man, but it does not follow that their evidence should be excluded entirely. The evidence furnished by a dog may lead to the conviction of a murderer, and although the Negro is below the white man in capabilities, there are exceptions.

Being thought of as a slave, and being compared to a dog, was an insult to African Americans, but they were thankful for any support, regardless of the reason. Atheneum members put their hearts and souls into the fourth campaign. They estimated that they talked to more than twenty-five thousand people. Gibbs and Lester alone talked to more than three thousand. The third petition had been signed by six hundred. The fourth was signed by more than five thousand, of whom approximately thirteen hundred were white. Considering the place and the period, it was an astounding number of white supporters.

When the legislature convened in April 1856, it was presented with the petition, a stack of papers six inches high. A number of law-makers favored the change in order to benefit whites, so this time the petition was received. But most still opposed black testimony for any reason and wouldn't allow debate. They sent the fourth petition to a committee where it was tabled and killed. Gibbs reacted with bitterness: "They laid our petition on the table," he said, "with the understanding that it was to be 'taken up' by the janitor."

Word of the defeat reached African Americans by way of the *Mirror of the Times,* the first black newspaper in California. It was started in 1856 by Gibbs, Lester, Jonas Townsend, and William Newby, Townsend and Newby being the principal writers. Gibbs never said what options were considered by the Atheneum following the latest defeat, but members surely held a meeting to discuss the subject. The Atheneum had never been just a room filled with books. It had always been a place for leaving the past, and it was filled with courage. After the defeat, the men issued a call for the Second State Convention of Colored Citizens of California to start on December 9, 1856.

This time, sixty-four delegates from seventeen counties filed into Barney Fletcher's church. This time, Jonas Townsend again banged the convention to order with extreme difficulty. Gibbs and Lester were seated toward the front to lend support to their friend and the new chairman, William Hall. Talking and arguing continued as Hall banged his gavel louder and harder until everyone sat down. The goal of the convention hadn't changed, but this meeting wasn't anything like the first.

William Hall was born a free man in New York and was self-educated. Like Gibbs, he had worked in the Underground Railroad in his youth, and he had worked to raise funds for a monument honoring Benjamin Banneker, a black mathematician and writer during the time of the American Revolution. Unlike Yates before him, Hall sensed the frustration of the delegates and let them speak on many subjects: the need for more schools, the need for their own bank, violence against blacks, and the injustice of slavery. After they vented their feelings for a day, the convention erupted in shouting over a statement by William Newby. On the subject of protecting America from a foreign invasion, Newby had exclaimed,

> Shall we say, "We will protect against foreign invasion!" God knows I speak advisedly—I would welcome an invasion by a foreign army, if that army provided liberty to me and my people in bondage! I speak the same words as the patriot Patrick Henry—"Give me liberty or give me death!"

Delegates shot up to agree and disagree. "Let the whites put away their prejudice and make us feel a part of this country," one yelled, "and then we will defend it!" Gibbs was sympathetic with the anger. But fearing a backlash from whites, he pleaded for calm, saying, "Let us not do anything that will increase the prejudices we face and hurt our cause." It didn't do any good. Hall's decision to allow a wide-ranging discussion had backfired for the moment, and the day ended with delegates standing on benches and shouting.

Order was restored the next morning, perhaps because delegates had had a good night's sleep and a chance to think about what they had done, or perhaps because they had had the opportunity to speak out on the previous day. By prior agreement, a resolution to suppress all matters not related to testimony was passed without objection. Later, resolutions for voting rights were adopted with little debate, and a committee was appointed to conduct the petition campaign of 1857. It included representatives from Napa, Sonoma, and San Mateo counties, which had not previously been involved.

The second convention did more than continue the fight for testimony. By allowing delegates to speak freely, Hall allowed them to feel like men—not like dogs begging for a bone. "There was a certain majesty in the chaos," Gibbs said, "and all felt like men, proud of who we were and what we had accomplished." His sentiments were reflected in William Hall's closing address, which took Gibbs back to 1849, when his inner voice had said, "Go do some great thing!" Rousing the group to action, William Hall declaimed,

> I urge each one of you to instruct our white brothers to remove their prejudices and recognize the intelligence and achievements of our race in this state. Talk with our ignorant white brethren, those who despise the poor Negro because he is a Negro, and show them that we do not deserve to be oppressed and denied the protection of the law. Talk with those who hold power about the injustice with which we are treated. Take their minds back to the days of childhood, when neither white or black knew any difference, when each heart was innocent. Remind them that this is what God intended! Appeal to their goodness and love of our country that we should no longer bear the yoke of servitude but be treated as men!
>
> Go forth, as members of the great race that we are! Tell your oppressor that he is not free who hates a man he does not know! Tell him that no man is free who denies God in his heart! Tell him that God weeps

because His children suffer! Go now, and do some great thing!

During the first three months of 1857, Gibbs and his fellow workers again approached strangers and appealed to their sense of fairness. How much ridicule they took will never be known, for they only talked about victories. How much money they lost by being away from business will never be known either, but for Gibbs and Lester it was a full-time job. By the close of the campaign, the workers had collected sixty-five hundred signatures, including twenty-five hundred from whites. The stack of papers, now eight inches high, was presented to the legislature in March 1857. It was sent to a committee and killed.

There was worse news to follow. On March 6, 1857, the United States Supreme Court issued the "Dred Scott Decision," the most famous Supreme Court decision involving slavery.

Dred Scott was a slave in Missouri. After his owner had taken him to the state of Illinois, Dred Scott sued for his freedom. He claimed that since Illinois was a free state, he should be free. The Court ruled that Dred Scott was still a slave, even in Illinois. He was still a slave because he was property, like a wagon, and citizens have the right to take property with them anywhere. The decision meant that slavery could exist anywhere, and slaves entering California needn't be disguised as employees anymore. Making no distinction between slaves and free African Americans, Chief Justice Roger Taney said, "Negroes have no rights which the white man is bound to respect."

Gibbs called Dred Scott "the worst decision in American history" and said its purpose was to spread slavery throughout America. The *Mirror of the Times* said, "Man was made in the image of God and no law can make him property!" Newby added, "The Colored People of California will not be silenced by the slavepower

Dred Scott.

and its allies in the Supreme Court." The Atheneum issued another call for action.

The Third State Convention of Colored Citizens of California met on October 13, 1857. It was held in the African Methodist Church in San Francisco, which had been started by James Starkey of the *Pocahontas*. Seventy delegates from eighteen counties attended, but no record of the proceedings has survived. Because William Hall was again chairman, delegates were probably allowed to vent. Probably things got out of hand from time to time and surely there were resolutions, including one denouncing the Dred Scott Decision. The purpose of the convention was made clear after it ended. Starting in January 1858, Gibbs and friends began collecting signatures for a sixth petition.

❖ EIGHT
Hurry Freedom

When Mifflin Gibbs took to the streets in 1858, San Francisco was hit with downpours of rain and its stores were often crowded with people seeking shelter. He said he avoided these places, knowing that the owners wouldn't tolerate his presence in such a situation; it was better when the store was empty or nearly so. Wearing wet clothes and shoes caked in mud, he referred to this period in his life as "trying to dig out from a deep hole where the ground keeps giving way." It was an understatement for any year in the gold rush period, but especially for 1858, when a string of events threatened to end the dreams of black forty-niners once and for all.

It started with an event that attracted little public notice but that angered the owners of the Boot Emporium. In 1857, Sarah Lester, Peter Lester's daughter, had taken the examination for admission to San Francisco's only high school. Her scores were second highest in general studies and highest in music and art. Sarah was so light-skinned that the authorities thought she was white and admitted her. A year later, in an anonymous letter to the school, her race was revealed and she was forced to withdraw. Sarah's rejection hardened her father. Gibbs remarked, "The school wouldn't be tainted with one ounce of Negro blood. It might disrupt studies." Many pupils in the school were Sarah's friends, and being separated from them hurt her the most.

Next came the ordeal of Archy Lee, which produced the most famous slave case in California history. Lee was eighteen and the slave of Charles Stovell, who brought him to Sacramento and hired him out. Lee ran and hid in the Hackett Hotel, which was owned by blacks, and Stovell had Lee arrested as a fugitive slave.

California's fugitive slave law had expired in 1855, so Lee's fate would be determined by the Dred Scott Decision, which said that owners could take slaves to free states but only if they were visiting and not if they were permanent residents. Stovell claimed to be a visitor, even though he had purchased property and taught school for several months in Sacramento. For African Americans, Archy Lee was the climax of an eight-year struggle against slavery in California. While Gibbs and Lester were trying to collect signatures in the rain, they sent $8,000 to Sacramento to fight for Lee's freedom. The Atheneum spent $50,000 on his case.

On January 26, 1858, a lower court ruled that Lee was free; Stovell was considered a permanent resident. He had Lee arrested again and appealed to the California Supreme Court, whose chief justice was David Terry, a fierce defender of slavery. The decision came on February 11: slavery was illegal in California, and people planning to settle in the state couldn't bring slaves in, but since Stovell didn't know about the law and was in poor health, Archy Lee was still his slave. News of the verdict triggered fights on the street in front of the courtroom. Blacks, whites, abolitionists, and defenders of slavery suffered cuts and bruises, and some went to jail.

As Stovell was leaving the state with Lee, workers in the Underground Railroad rescued Lee and hid him, maybe in Barney Fletcher's church. During the next two months, Lee was rearrested and rescued four times while his case was heard before different judges and commissioners. The rulings dominated the news and led to more fights.

Lee finally won his freedom on April 14, but at a high cost to African Americans. Newspapers criticized them for "kidnapping" Lee and fighting with whites. Gibbs answered the charge in a letter to the *San Francisco Bulletin:*

There has been an inclination by the press to misinterpret us by characterizing us as rebellious people who disregard

the law. We wish to inform the public that we are a law-
abiding class of people, even though we are governed by
unjust laws. It has been asserted that we have kidnapped
the boy Archy from officers and have broken the law. We
pronounce this a falsehood. We feel that we are maintaining
the laws of the state of California and ask for the boy's liberation on just and legal grounds. He is entitled to his
freedom, and we will leave no proper means untried to
see that slavery will not be tolerated where it has been
declared illegal.

Although Archy Lee was a victory for African Americans, the case
didn't end slavery in California. Slaves continued to arrive: their
owners pretended either that they were employees or that they
themselves were just visiting. Slaves ran and were caught, but
there wasn't enough money to fight all the cases and fight the testimony law as well. In the same month that Archy Lee won his freedom, the sixth petition arrived in Sacramento, a pile of papers
smeared by rain but signed by sixty-five hundred people. It was
sent to committee and killed. Meanwhile, the legislature had pre-
pared a response to Lee's freedom.

The constitutional convention of 1849 had called for a ban on
blacks' entering California. During every session of the legislature
from 1850 to 1857, laws barring blacks had been proposed and
defeated, so slaves could still enter the state. Now that the Archy
Lee case had demonstrated that slaves could become free in
California, the legislature was moved to act with Assembly Bill 339:
"An Act to Restrict and Prevent the Immigration to and Residence
in the State of Negroes and Mulattoes." The white backlash that
Gibbs had feared was upon them in the form of a new and hate-
filled law.

The bill prohibited all African Americans from entering the

state. Those who tried would be deported at their own expense. If they didn't have the money, the state would assume the role of slave owner and hire them out until they had the money to leave. For those already in the state working for freedom money, the bill meant that their families couldn't be brought to California. African Americans already in the state had to register as "Negroes" by October 1, 1858. Any who refused would be sold to the highest bidder for six months' work followed by deportation. "Registered Negroes" had to obtain a special license to run a business, and employing an "unlicensed Negro" was punishable by a fine.

The bill cast Gibbs back to the time when life seemed futile. Battling the Panama jungle, being shut out from carpentry work, bootblacking, clerking, and finally ending up as a business owner with enough money to fight slavery and fight for the right of testimony—all seemed useless. Suppose he was able to obtain a special license and continue with the Boot Emporium. He couldn't picture himself fitting a customer with shoes and rising up with the word *Negro* emblazoned across his forehead. This was not what Gibbs wanted out of the gold rush. He wanted to go forward, not backward. He wanted to be valued as a human being. The bill was a kick to his head, spit on his face, and was the low point for black forty-niners and for California.

On April 13, 1858, the assembly passed the bill by a vote of forty-five to eight and sent it to the senate. After eight years, six petitions, and three conventions, Mifflin Gibbs let out his anger in a letter to the *San Francisco Bulletin:*

Let the bill now before the legislature take what turn it may.
The colored people in this state have no regrets to offer. Our
course has been manly and law-abiding. To this legislature
and the press that sustains it, may you have all the honor,
glory and consequences of prosecuting and abusing an

industrious, unoffending and defenseless people! May God
have shame on you! Shame! May He judge you for your
actions! Shame! Shame!

The year also saw increasing violence against blacks. As Archy
Lee's case unfolded and the other events occurred, there were two
attempts to burn down the African Methodist Church in San
Francisco and one attempt to burn the African Methodist Church in
Sacramento. In Stockton a mob attacked three homes occupied by
blacks, and in Marysville a tailor shop was burned to the ground.
The *Sacramento Union* said in 1858 that the Dred Scott Decision and
the exclusion bill gave whites "the liberty to do as they pleased to
Negroes."

Two days after the exclusion bill passed the assembly, a crowd of
five hundred gathered in San Francisco at the suggestion of the
Atheneum. Archy Lee was introduced and received loud applause,
but there were no speeches about slavery or the need for testimony.
The purpose of the gathering was to discuss plans for leaving
California, as the future did not look good for African Americans
there. Panama and Mexico were mentioned as places where they
might relocate, but they settled on Victoria, British Columbia,
Canada, where gold had been discovered and where everyone had
equal protection under the law. Most in the crowd vowed that they
would go.

The conventions stopped, the petitions stopped, plans were
made to leave. Barbershops were offered for sale. Restaurants were
abandoned and marked with signs reading "Gone to Victoria." The
Hackett Hotel, where Archy Lee had hidden, was sold. In March,
the *Mirror of the Times* ceased publication.

On April 22, more than two hundred left for Victoria on the
steamer *Commodore,* including Archy Lee. More would follow, and
approximately nine hundred left altogether, reducing California's

black population by nearly a fifth and San Francisco's by one half. Half of the Atheneum's membership migrated and it was sold and converted to a restaurant.

Gibbs and Lester sold the Boot Emporium and left on the *Commodore* when it sailed in April. Gibbs took two trunks of possessions and a bundle of cash, and as the ship sailed out of the bay, he recalled the events that had led to his leaving California, most notably the exclusion bill and the failure to achieve testimony. His trunks and cash were indicators of his success in California, but certain images never faded from his mind: Lester's beating, and the stares he received while trying to collect signatures. As the city faded in the distance, he thought about the friends he was leaving behind and what they might face in the future.

Only hours before, he had been chosen to deliver a farewell

The steamer Commodore *enters Victoria, British Columbia, in July 1858, carrying gold seekers from California. Gibbs and Lester were among the many African Americans who took the* Commodore *north to Canada.*

Victoria, British Columbia, in 1858.

address to African Americans who had gathered to see the migrants off. Gibbs told them the truth: California had given them a new chance at life and they should be thankful. But he was bitter over what might have been, and he spoke from the heart. "God knows we have tried to live in this state," he said. "We have worked next to the white man, and worked as hard as any race, to show that we are part of the human family. We have tried, but it is time to find a new home where we might live in peace." With that, he said good-bye, not knowing that in his eight years in California he had indeed done a great thing for himself and for generations to come.

The exclusion bill never became law. It passed the senate with amendments, but too many members of the assembly were drunk and unable to vote before the legislature adjourned. Still, with more than a fifth of the black population having already left, the bill had had the same effect as if it had passed: intimidation.

But one event never stopped. On the first Sunday of August in 1858, a crowd of three hundred assembled in San Francisco to make a noise for freedom. Minus a brass band, they marched and sang anti-slavery songs, and afterward the Reverend Samuel Tripp, from Sacramento, led them in prayer:

Hear us, O Lord! How long must we wait for freedom? While our brothers and sisters toil for their masters, we have endeavored to rise up from slavery and to show that our race was not meant for bondage. We have made a home for ourselves in a distant place, but until the chains are broken, and the yoke of slavery removed from us, we are not free. When is the day of our liberation? How long must we wait for freedom? Blessed will be that day when we can live without shame because of the color of our skin! When slavery has ended, as it must, the white man will see that we are a mighty race, capable of many great things, and that we are part of humanity!

O Lord! When is the hour of our deliverance? How long must we wait for freedom?

❖ NINE
Freedom

Reverend Tripp's question had been asked since the first slave arrived in America in 1619. Over the next two hundred and fifty years, countless people were born and died as slaves without getting an answer. Families were separated, their African culture was destroyed, and slavery became part of the Constitution. From George Washington to Thomas Jefferson to Andrew Jackson, many notable Americans owned slaves, and slavery had always been an important part of the economy. So Tripp's question had no easy answer, even though in 1858 Cuba, Brazil, and the United States were the only nations that still had slavery.

When the question was finally answered, Gibbs and Lester were in British Columbia. Gibbs kept his subscription to the *North Star* and followed the events that led to the end of slavery in the United States. He was surprised at how freedom came. From his point of view, it came for the wrong reason, and if he cherished the moment, he didn't celebrate the way slavery ended. Imagine him sitting on a bench in a park reading about the events as they occurred.

By 1858, the North and South were locked in conflict over the expansion of slavery into the western territories. Representing the North, the Republican Party pledged to stop the spread of slavery. The Democrats in the South claimed the action was illegal because only states had power over slavery. After Abraham Lincoln and the Republicans won the election in 1860, most of the slave states seceded from the Union, causing the outbreak of the American Civil War in 1861.

The war wasn't fought to end slavery. At the start of the war President Lincoln said, "I will not interfere with slavery in the states where it exists." The abolitionists knew this and so did Gibbs. They agreed with Frederick Douglass, who wrote at the start of the conflict, "The Negro will never benefit from the war." To the North and the Republicans, the war was fought to keep slaves and African Americans out of the western territories. The Republicans called their party "the white man's party" and favored barring all blacks from the territories, much as California had with its exclusion bill.

Eventually, the Civil War changed Lincoln's thinking. After two years of fighting, he came to realize that to defeat the South and shorten the war, he had to attack slavery. Slavery was the South's greatest resource and slaves supplied the army.

Lincoln also wanted to keep Great Britain out of the war. Lincoln's navy had put a blockade around the southern states, cutting off the supply of cotton to British textile mills. Great Britain wanted to get its cotton and threatened to break the blockade and enter the war on the side of the South. But Great Britain also wanted the United States to abolish slavery. By attacking slavery, Lincoln could keep Great Britain out of the war and increase the North's chance of victory.

Accordingly, in January 1863, Lincoln issued the Emancipation Proclamation. It declared that slaves in disloyal states were free. It didn't actually free these slaves because the northern army didn't control the disloyal states. And because it did not apply to the four slave states loyal to the Union, the Emancipation Proclamation didn't in fact free any slaves. The *North Star* criticized the Proclamation: "The principle is not that a human being cannot own another, but that he cannot own him unless he is loyal to the United States." Gibbs agreed as he read about the riots in northern cities that resulted from the Proclamation. Whites refused to fight in a war to end slavery and burned black neighborhoods, including parts of his birthplace, Philadelphia.

President Lincoln reads the Emancipation Proclamation to his Cabinet, January 1863.

The Emancipation Proclamation made the Civil War a war to end slavery, which few could have predicted in 1861. In 1864, Congress passed the Thirteenth Amendment to the Constitution, which abolished slavery, and in 1865 the South was defeated and the Thirteenth Amendment became law. Just like that, in two short years, slavery was gone. Gibbs knew it was abolished to win the war and not because there had been a change in attitude toward African Americans. Lincoln knew it, too. But reasons aside, four million African Americans were free, and from now on the enemy was race prejudice, which wouldn't fade soon.

Throughout the Civil War, newspapers in California ridiculed the idea that blacks were suited for freedom. They denounced the

"War for the Negroes" and wrote jingles to arouse the public:

> The Darkies and Republicans
> Have more than they can do,
> Abolition grease
> Won't slip the Negro through.
>
> The Constitution as it is,
> The Union as it was—
> The Darkies in the cotton field
> The Clergy preaching God.

In the face of this harsh language, the abolition of slavery was celebrated in California inside black churches, where the songs and prayers were louder than ever. At the end of the war, Barney Fletcher's congregation met and the Reverend Fletcher shouted, "Thank God Almighty! A stain has been lifted from the fabric of the nation. . . . Freedom! Freedom! Freedom!" Meanwhile, others had renewed the campaign for testimony.

In 1861, William Hall and former Atheneum members met with leaders of California's Republican Party to discuss black testimony. Their biggest supporter was Caleb Fay, the white lawyer who bought slaves and gave them their freedom and who was now a member of the legislature. The Republicans were divided on the issue and were in a minority in the legislature. When they won control of the legislature in 1863, Hall and the others came back. In January, they presented Republicans with the seventh petition for testimony. Although it contained only six hundred signatures, to the men who collected the names, this stack of papers represented the work of all the previous petitions.

The resulting bill passed the senate on January 30 by a vote of twenty-two to fourteen. It passed the assembly on March 10 by

Document signed by the California legislature in 1865 ratifying the Thirteenth Amendment to the United States Constitution, abolishing slavery.

a vote of forty-six to thirty-one. Together with people like Caleb Fay, who had fought for a change in the law since 1851, most law-makers voted "yes" because the abolition of slavery was now one of the goals of the Civil War and former slaves would need the right of testimony to protect themselves. On March 18, 1863, Governor Leland Stanford signed the bill into law and the victory was complete. It was an item that received little attention in news-papers—but it was monumental to those affected by the change.

In 1862, Phillip Bell had started the *Pacific Appeal* in San Francisco, the second black newspaper in California. It was avail-able in Victoria, where Gibbs, Lester, and Archy Lee read news of the victory. Gibbs must have smiled and shaken his head. Lester probably reached for the scar on the back of his neck. The *Pacific Appeal* carried the news to Hartwell Bates, the former cowboy who now owned his own ranch in Stockton, and to Sol Eaton and his wife, who were still cooking in Negro Tent, which by now had six employees. A great fear had been vanquished from their lives and they had brought about the change. With the change in the testi-mony law in 1863 and passage of the Fourteenth Amendment to the Constitution in 1868, granting citizenship to African Americans, they were guaranteed equal protection under the law.

African Americans postponed a public celebration until the end of the Civil War. On October 25, 1865, they met at the Fourth State Convention of Colored Citizens of California, held in the African Methodist Church in San Francisco. Delegates came from all over the state to celebrate the end of slavery, the change in the testimony law, and the progress of African Americans in California. The songs they sang had echoed on the streets of San Francisco for more than fifteen years, as had their prayers for freedom. Now they gave thanks for prayers answered.

William Hall was chairman again. As he gazed at the people packed in the church, he must have reflected back to previous work, to Mifflin Gibbs and Peter Lester, to all the signatures the three had collected, to the Atheneum, to the conventions, to Archy Lee, and to the Railroad. Maybe he even recalled dodging bullets shot by the members of a mining association way back in 1850 when he first arrived in California. It would have been appropriate.

In his address, Hall denounced the injustice of slavery and thanked those who had brought it to an end. He praised those whites who had fought against slavery in the state and backed the fight for civil rights. They endured the same ridicule as blacks, Hall said, and he called them "friends in time of need." He spoke of "emerging from the darkness of a long night into the bright beams of a dawning day" and urged further changes if they were to achieve true equality with whites. His voice ever strong, he ended by praising gold rush California for "fulfilling our dreams and providing hope for generations to come."

❖ EPILOGUE

Mifflin Gibbs arrived in Victoria with his cash and trunks secure. After sizing up the place, he opened a merchandising store and earned $1,000 in his first month. Next, he bought several houses, rented them, and invested in the coal industry, which had just started. Gibbs finally found a wife, an educated woman named Maria Alexander. They married and had a son and two daughters. Gibbs bought a fancy buggy to carry the family around in, which was fitting for a prominent citizen of the city.

As before, he was outgoing and made many friends. African Americans and whites elected Gibbs councilman from James Bay in Victoria, a position that he seemed to enjoy. By 1867, a construction company he owned had built a railroad, and he had been named superintendent. His railroad shipped the first coal mined on the Pacific Coast.

Peter Lester bought a hotel in Victoria, which he ran successfully for years. Archy Lee invested in real estate and became wealthy. James Starkey, who had first come to California to earn enough money to buy his wife and children out of slavery, finally returned to the South from British Columbia. His wife had died, but he located his children through advertisements in the black press.

Meanwhile, those who had made their homes in Canada found themselves fighting the same old fight: besides African Americans, thousands of whites had left California for British Columbia, carrying their prejudices with them. In 1860, a group of African Americans tried to attend the lavish Colonial Theater but were attacked by whites. The brawl lasted an hour, until police arrived and cleared the theater.

Those who stayed behind in California prospered as well. William Hall's billiard parlor remained profitable and George Washington Dennis expanded his livery stable business, his father having long since gone broke in running the Eldorado Hotel. During the Civil War, Jeremiah Sanderson raised funds for black troops fighting in the Union Army and Barney Fletcher organized the Black Woman's Beneficial Society to help destitute women.

Gibbs left Victoria in 1869 with the goal of becoming a lawyer. He enrolled in Oberlin College in Ohio and later moved to Arkansas, where he was admitted to the bar in 1870, at the age of 47. In 1873, he was elected City Judge for Little Rock, Arkansas, and he served as Registrar of Lands in Arkansas from 1877 to 1884. Bootblacking and an inner voice had given him a start, and from his first years in California he never looked back. In the 1890s, Mifflin Wistar Gibbs was the United States Ambassador to the African nation of Madagascar. It was a long road traveled to a fitting end and a lesson well learned: history has a knack for justice.

❖ BIBLIOGRAPHIC NOTE

The poverty and prejudice that African Americans faced in the North is documented in Melvin Drimmer, *Black History: A Reappraisal* (New York: Doubleday, 1969); Philip S. Foner, *History of Black Americans from the Emergence of the Cotton Kingdom to the Eve of the Compromise of 1850* (Westport, Connecticut: Greenwood Press, 1983); John Hope Franklin, *From Slavery to Freedom: A History of Negro Americans* (New York: Alfred A. Knopf, 6th ed., 1988); Leon Litwack, *North of Slavery: The Negro in the Free States, 1790–1860* (Chicago: University of Chicago Press, 1965); and August Meier and Elliott Rudwick, *From Plantation to Ghetto* (New York: Hill and Wang, 3rd ed., 1976).

The following sources were used to trace the life of Mifflin Gibbs: Tom W. Dillard, "The Black Moses of the West: A Biography of Mifflin Wistar Gibbs, 1823–1915" (M.A. Thesis, University of Arkansas, 1975); Tom W. Dillard, "'Golden Prospects and Fraternal Amenities': Mifflin W. Gibbs's Arkansas Years," in *The Arkansas Historical Quarterly* (Winter 1976), pp. 307–333; Mifflin Wistar Gibbs, *Shadow and Light: An Autobiography* (New York: Arno Press and the *New York Times*, 1968); "Colored Man Was a Judge," *Little Rock Gazette*, August 24, 1903; and "Mifflin Wistar Gibbs Called by Death," *Little Rock Gazette*, July 12, 1915.

Information concerning the migration of African Americans to California and their history during the gold rush came from: Delilah L. Beasley, *The Negro Trail Blazers of California* (Los Angeles: R and E Research Associates, 1919); Delilah L. Beasley, "Slavery in California," in *Journal of Negro History* (January 1918), pp. 33–44; Howard H. Bell, "The Negro in California, 1849–1859," in *Phylon* (Summer 1967), pp. 151–60; Eugene H. Berwanger, *The Frontier Against Slavery: Anti-Negro Prejudice and the Slavery Extension Controversy* (Urbana, Illinois: University of Illinois Press, 1967); Kenneth G. Godde, *California's Black Pioneers: A Brief Historical Survey* (Santa Barbara, California: McNally and Loftin, 1974); William L. Katz, *The Black West* (New York: Doubleday, 1971); Rudolph M. Lapp, *Blacks in Gold Rush California* (New Haven, Connecticut: Yale University Press, 1977); W.

Sherman Savage, *Blacks in the West* (Westport, Connecticut: Greenwood Press, 1976); W. Sherman Savage, "The Negro in the Westward Movement," in *Journal of Negro History* (October 1940), pp. 531–39; and Sue B. Thurman, *Pioneers of Negro Origin in California* (San Francisco: Acme Publishing, 1949).

Information related to the struggle for civil rights came from: Robert J. Chandler, "Friends in Time of Need: Republicans and Black Civil Rights in California During the Civil War Era," in *Arizona and the West* (Winter 1982), pp. 319–40; James A. Fisher, "The Struggle for Negro Testimony," in *Southern California Quarterly* (December 1969), pp. 313–24; Philip S. Foner and George E. Walker, eds., *Proceedings of the Black State Conventions, 1840–1865*, Vol. 2 (Philadelphia: Temple University Press, 1980); William F. Franklin, "The Archy Case," in *Pacific Historical Review* (May 1963), pp. 137–54; Mifflin Wistar Gibbs, *Shadow and Light;* Rudolph M. Lapp, *Archy Lee: A California Fugitive Slave Case* (San Francisco: Book Club of California, 1969); Rudolph M. Lapp, "Jeremiah B. Sanderson: Early California Negro Leader," in *Journal of Negro History* (May 1968), pp. 137–54; Rudolph M. Lapp, "Negro Rights Activities in Gold Rush California," in *California Historical Society Quarterly* (March 1966), pp. 3–20; and B. Gordon Wheeler, *Black California: The History of African Americans in the Golden State* (New York: Hippocrene Books, 1993).

For the African American exodus to Victoria, see: F. W. Howay, "The Negro Immigration into Vancouver Island in 1858," in *British Columbia Historical Quarterly* (Fall 1939), pp. 101–13; Crawford Killian, *Go Do Some Great Thing: The Black Pioneers of British Columbia* (Vancouver, British Columbia: Douglas & McIntyre, 1978); and James W. Pilton, "Negro Settlement in B.C., 1858–1971" (M.A. Thesis, University of British Columbia, 1951).

Tom W. Dillard of the Butler Center for Arkansas Studies in Little Rock, Arkansas, Lynn Ewbank of the Arkansas History Commission in Little Rock, Arkansas, and the Oberlin College Archives in Oberlin, Ohio, provided additional research. Derisive terms from the period used to describe African Americans have been changed and some quotations were edited for clarity.

❖ INDEX

❖ PICTURE CREDITS